Published by Enterprise Management Limited

For information contact info@enterprisemgt.com

Copyright © 2017 by Mary B. Lippitt. All rights reserved in whole or part in all forms of media. No part of this book may be reproduced, stored in a retrieval system or transmitted in any form or by any means, electronic, mechanical, photocopying, recording, or otherwise, without written permission of the publisher. Violation of the copyright held herein subjects the infringer to civil and criminal penalties, including statutory damages and applicable fines.

The Leadership Spectrum Profile is a registered trademark of Enterprise Management Limited.

Special discounts on bulk purchases of Enterprise Management Limited books and materials are available to corporations, associations and other organization. For details contact info@enterprisemgt.com.

Published in the United States of America

ISBN 978-0-9715907-9-3

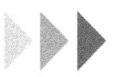# Introduction

Readers of Brilliant or Blunder: 6 Ways Leaders Navigate Uncertainty, Opportunity and Complexity have asked for additional information on how to use Mindset mastery to successfully handle change, make smarter decisions, and develop mental nimbleness in others. The first six chapters of this book offer practical advice and are organized to help you discover and improve your ability to leverage a specific Situational Mindset. The final chapter moves beyond an individual Mindset to explore how the framework boosts influencing, conflict management and team building.

The six Situational Mindset specific chapters describes the point of view and offers suggestions on how to apply the Mindset effectively.

Sections in the six Situational Mindset chapters include:

- An overview of the Mindset through reflection on the circumstance when you have used the Mindset, tips to encourage others to use it, and the potential barriers that may impede its use.
- Exercise 1 identifies tools, practices or processes that support the use of the specific Mindset.
- Exercise 2 outlines a thinking process used to apply the Mindset. A practice situaion is offered at the conclusion of the steps. This situation enables you to practice the steps to improve retention and be comfortable explaining the steps to others.
- Exercise 3 provides an opportunity to apply the Mindset to one of your current work situations or issues.
- Exercise 4: describes a situation where influence is needed. This exercise enables you to seamlessly detect and tailor your approach to a person operating from another perspective.

The final chapter explores how to work with multiple Mindsets to influence up the chain of command, manage disagreements and conflict, and enhance team effectiveness.

I want to thank my clients, students, and colleagues for their input into this guide. I hope you find it valuable.

If you have questions, suggestions, or comments please contact me at mlippitt@enterprisemgt.com. I look forward to hearing from you.

Dr. Mary Lippitt

▶▶▶ Situational Mindsets

Brilliant or Blunder presents the importance of situational Mindsets. The **Leadership Spectrum Profile®** enhances our ability to choose what information we collect and evaluate. A leader must master the ability to work with conflicting data so they can base their actions on current internal and external realities. Evidence and context count. Successful leaders effectively collect evidence, evaluate opportunities and manage change. Failure to consider current data creates blind spots that overlook key ramifications, potential risks and other barriers. We cannot rely on habit and past practice in a fast changing world.

Mindset is defined as a:

- Filter used to collect and evaluate information
- Point of view, assumption or frame of reference for making decisions
- Perspective, attitude or mental state toward a issue
- Approach to a current situation

While some use the word mindset to describe an attitude or belief system, ***Brilliant or Blunder's*** definition concentrates on organizational variables to deliver sound decision making, action planning and effective risk management. When situations shift, issues are complex, data is ambiguous or when faced with a precedent setting decision, it is important to collect information from all six Situational Mindsets before deciding what is most important to achieve first given current circumstances.

The six *Situational* Mindsets focus on different key organizational questions:

Inventing: What new products or services can we offer?
How can we leverage technology?

Catalyzing: What can help us grow and compete?
How can we improve customer service?

Developing: How should we organize? What policies should guide our decisions?

Performing: How can we increase efficiencies? How can we improve quality?

Protecting: How can we retain key talent?
What will sustain a high-performing culture?

Challenging: What trends can we leverage? What assumptions need to be tested?

©2017. Enterprise Management Ltd. All Rights Reserved.

Mental agility is crucial when dealing with change, complexity and precedent setting situations in our rapidly changing work environment. Overlooking key data in one of the Mindsets creates unnecessary risks and potential failure. Leaders must be able to detect environmental shifts, discover new opportunities and identify potential pitfalls. Learning the tools to make smarter decisions depends on measuring current reality.

Mindset Priorities is the most pressing *Situational* Mindset at a point in time. They are also:

- Subject to rapid change to cope with new information and circumstances
- Identify the most pressing goal or desired outcome
- Guide execution planning
- Improve the allocation of time & resources

The following exercises, processes, and knowledge gained will enable you to enhance your ability to effectively manage complexity, implement change and develop critical thinking skills in others.

Identifying Mindsets with Mindset Predictor

Mindsets also enable you to identify what goals drive others. As you listen to others speak about what they want or what they like to avoid, you can predict which Mindset is currently driving their thinking for that situation. Check the Considers Valuable column for those outcomes that are currently being sought and the Impediments column for issues that they are trying to avoid or consider a barrier to achieving their goal. Remember that there may be two or more Mindsets driving an individual. The following descriptions can be used as a guide to identify the current driving Mindset. Please refer to the Predictor on the next page.

MINDSET PREDICTOR	CONSIDERS VALUABLE	IMPEDIMENTS
INVENTING	Exploration of new options Discretionary time to pursue ideas Systems that reward innovation, Challenging tasks Discovering new synergies	Excessive structure Tight deadlines Routine assignments Short term thinking Resistance to new ideas
CATALYZING	"Can do" orientation Flexibility Personal persuasion Sales growth Customer knowledge	Slow decision making Process details Fear of rapid growth Lack of commitment Lost time, delay
DEVELOPING	Establish goals and systems Seamless execution Macro viewpoint Roles and responsiblities Structure and policies	Confusion or chaos Tangential thinking Ineffective systems Inadequate operational analysis Lack of clear responsibilities
PERFORMING	Quality Reliance on data and metrics Workflow improvements Efficiency and ROI Process knowledge	Missing or withheld information Subjectivity Sub-optimization or "turfdom" Performance gaps Inattention to the "bottom line"
PROTECTING	High performing culture Risk analysis Tradition and sense of community Talent development Succession planning	Change for the sake of change Unwarranted risk Conflict Failure to follow established procedures Short term orientation
CHALLENGING	Future orientation Reflection and lessons learned Trend analysis New business models Assumption testing	Missed opportunities Resistance to new perspectives Lack of strategic focus Reliance on the status quo Ignoring trends

Mindset Match

To practice your Mindset detection effectiveness, match the comments below with the likely Mindset Priority in the statements below. Given these short statements, more than one Mindset might apply. As a guide, you can refer to prior page or the Mindset Checklist on pages 66-68. Please record Inv for Inventing, Cat for Catalyzing, Dev for Developer, Per for Performing, Pro for Protecting and Chal for Challenging next to each statement.

_____ 1. We have to get everyone committed to getting the job done.

_____ 2. We should not change for the sake of change because our traditions are important to maintaining our high performing culture.

_____ 3. We need to clarify roles and responsibilities since no one knows who is supposed to be doing what.

_____ 4. What can we do to reduce costs and increase productivity?

_____ 5. We need to revise our vision for the future.

_____ 6. How are we doing against the plan/schedule?

_____ 7. What is the newest thinking in that area?

_____ 8. We need to offer training and career development to retain talent.

_____ 9. What threats exist on the horizon?

_____ 10. The VP wants to gain market share and improve customer service..

_____ 11. What policies can ensure that we learn from experience and work across our units effectively?

_____ 12. We need to rethink our assumptions.

_____ 13. Let's think about creative options.

_____ 14. What gets measured gets done.

_____ 15. We need to incorporate new technology in our products to be known as a state of the art firm.

Answers are found on page 66.

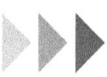 ## Understanding the Inventing Mindset

The Inventing Mindsets seeks to discover new products or services and leverage internal synergies. It concentrates on different perspectives, seeing new alternatives, applying technology in new ways, or seizing opportunities. It identifies creative ideas or processes using non-traditional approaches. The result may be a new process, service, or product such as the more effective mousetrap. Or it may be an improvement in the way services are fulfilled or a product is manufactured.

Years ago a *Ripley's Believe It or Not* story reported that a plain iron bar was worth $5.00. But forged into horseshoes, its value would be twice as much. And if made into needles, its value would soar to $3,285. Invention is often the difference between $5.00 and $3,285.

The human mind, once stretched to a new idea,
never goes back to its original dimension.
—OLIVER WENDELL HOLMES

Reflection

▸ What conditions stimulate your Inventing Mindset?
_____
_____

▸ What can you do to stimulate the Inventing Mindset in others?
_____
_____

The following practices stimulates the use of the Inventing Mindset:
▸ Focusing on the situation for a dedicated period of time
▸ Restating the problem from multiple perspectives
▸ Using analogies to trigger ideas in brainstorming sessions
▸ Employing metaphors, word association, or forced comparisons
▸ Conducting a brainstorming sessions
▸ Engaging in blue-sky thinking or day dreaming
▸ Posting storyboards for information and additional input
▸ Holding meetings away from daily distractions
▸ Visualizing what extraordinary success will look like in 10 years
▸ Ensuring diversity during brainstorming (tenure, function, expertise)

- Demonstrating respect and admiration for creative or critical thinking
- Setting an expectation that team members display critical, strategic or innovative thinking when discussing complex issues

It is also wise to address any potential barriers to the Inventing Mindset by:

- Removing any lack of confidence in the ability to be creative
- Addressing concerns that new ideas will mean a heavier workload
- Discussing the danger of staying with the tried and true
- Confirming that careers will be enhanced, not limited, by creative ideas
- Focusing on constraints (time, staff, budget, review cycle, workload etc.)

Exercise 1: Tools to Boost the Inventing Mindset

1. Groups can be either creative or they might beconstrained by passively accepting a traditional solution. To encourage innovative thinking, set aside a dedicated portion of a meeting (10 minutes or more) or an entire meeting. It is important to separate the invention process from the evaluation process or from jumping to conclusions.

Rules for brainstorming are:

- List every idea as stated, without evaluation, editing or judging.
- Assume that all ideas are valuable.
- Avoid digging into a suggestion or extended explanations. Clarifications may be needed.
- Accept silence, since many ideas flow from reflection.
- Hitchhiking, or using one idea as the basis for another, is acceptable and encouraged.

2. Stimulate discussion by asking:

- How could we improve . . . ?
- What would happen if . . . ?
- What alternatives should we consider?
- Who has an idea to kick-off our discussion?
- What ideas surfaced from past experiences and projects?
- What do we need to start doing, stop doing, do more often or do less often?
- How have you or others handled it in the past? What would you do differently?
- What trends present new options?
- What do we need to do to be a state-of-the-art firm?
- How can we revitalize or expand our products/services?

©2017. Enterprise Management Ltd. All Rights Reserved.

Exercise 2: Inventing Mindset Steps

Review the following steps to deploy the Inventing Mindsets. These steps will be used at the end to analyze a situation. The lines below each step are for your analysis.

1. Step One: Identify the issue clearly. Make it as broad as possible to ensure that you are not limiting alternatives. Take particular care that it does not appear to be an either/or statement or lead to just one alternative or solution.

   _____

   _____

2. Step Two: Use these questions to stimulate thinking:

   ▸ What ideas/options would surface if the reverse was being sought?

   _____

   _____

   ▸ How can existing processes, systems, or resources be adapted?

   _____

   _____

   ▸ How can standards be modified or altered to increase options?

   _____

   _____

   ▸ How can the scope be increased, decreased, modified ?

   _____

   _____

   ▸ What can technology offer?

   _____

   _____

© 2017. Enterprise Management Ltd. All Rights Reserved.

- Are substitutions an option?

  _____

  _____

- Can current practices be re-arranged, re-sequenced, or modified?

  _____

  _____

- Is a blend or combination of existing practices or systems an option?

  _____

  _____

3. Step Three: Ensure that you have at least four viable alternatives. If you are not able to identify four options, take a break and return to the project at another time or on another day. Time frequently surfaces new options.

   _____

   _____

4. Step Four: Develop criteria for evaluating the alternatives, including the level of support required for implementation.

   _____

   _____

5. Step Five: Evaluate the alternatives. Consider: cost to implement, time for results to be evident, resource consumption (management time, facilities, existing equipment), number of authorizations required, number of individuals needed for implementation, quantified impact or benefits, qualified impact (reputation, goodwill, morale), and other relevant standards.

Putting the Steps to Work: Analyze the Following Situation

Turnover has increased dramatically over the last six months impacting productivity, scheduling, and quality. The organization must retain millennial staff as well as more experienced managers since upper management succession is an issue with expected retirements. What causes might be contributing? What solutions are possible?

_____

Exercise 3: Applying the Inventing Mindset

1. Identify three situations or problems that exist right now in your organization. Select the issue that is most pressing, interesting, or offers the most promising impact.

   _____

   _____

2. Develop an initial approach by asking:

   ▸ What data is needed?

   _____

   _____

   ▸ Who needs to be consulted or included?

   _____

   _____

   ▸ How has it been handled in the past?

   _____

   _____

   ▸ What are the alternatives?

   _____

   _____

   ▸ What can technology offer?

   _____

   _____

▸ If we were starting over , or from scratch, what would we do?

_____

_____

▸ Who needs to authorize? Who needs to actively support this proposal?

_____

_____

▸ What are the desired benefits?

_____

_____

▸ What steps can be taken to advance the idea or move the ball forward?

_____

_____

3. Evaluate proposals on the basis of the following criteria: cost to implement, time for results to be evident, resource consumption (management time, facilities, existing equipment), number of authorizations required, number of individuals needed for implementation, new sills required, quantified impact or benefit, degree of change required, qualified impact (reputation, goodwill, morale), and other relevant standards.

_____

_____

_____

_____

_____

Exercise 4: Influencing an Inventing Mindset

What would you do to influence thinking in this situation?

An operations manager and her team have proposed changes in their organization structure to improve efficiencies. Their proposal highlighted reducing redundancies and costs based on their current Performing Mindset. The change would mean altering job classifications and shifting pay policy but the cost/benefit analysis was extremely positive. They developed a rational "bottom-line" presentation, assuming that it would be compelling usng the Performing Mindset. It was rejected. The manager and the team realized their proposal was not aligned with the VP's Inventing Mindset. The team elected to revamp their presentation to target the VP's current Inventin Mindset.

1. With your new understanding of the VP's Mindset, what three phrases below are most likely to interest the VP to approve the proposal:

    Fast growth, new markets, revolutionary, customer service, monitoring, systems, state-of-the-art, accountabilities, efficiency, standards, risk reduction, breakthrough, tradition, teamwork, competencies

2. Write an opening statement that highlights the Inventing Mindset to capture the VP's attention.

    _____

    _____

    _____

    _____

    _____

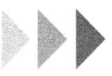 ## Understanding the Catalyzing Mindset

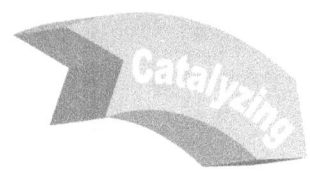

The Catalyzing Mindset focuses on customers, clients, and sponsors as key to success and rallies support for retaining and expanding the customer base. It targets effective sales strategy, negotiation, quick response times, customer service and surpassing the competition. In an effort to increase market share, the Catalyzing Mindset encourages others to take the initiative and act quickly to serve customers.

The Catalyzing Mindset recognizes that they have to stretch boundaries to meet today's demanding customers and competitive pressures.

"Making promises and keeping them is a great way to build a brand."
—SETH GODIN

Reflection
- What conditions stimulate your Catalyzing Mindset

  _____

  _____

- What can you do to stimulate the Catalyzing Mindset in others?

  _____

  _____

The following stimulates the Catalyzing Mindset:
- Communicating regularly with valued customers and asking for feedback
- Staying alert to key competitors
- Knowing trends that will impact the market
- Tracking market share
- Establishing customer feedback mechanisms including surveys
- Visiting with key customers
- Monitoring potential new market segments
- Rewarding those who display outstanding customer service
- Recognizing those who take initiative
- Monitoring your reputation and brand
- Motivating others to respond quickly to opportunities and threats

It is also wise to address any potential barriers to the Catalyzing Mindset caused by:

- Ignoring market share changes
- Relying on "cash cows" without developing a product pipeline
- Assuming the inferiority of your competition
- Believing that all customers are equally valuable
- Ignoring customer complaints, returns, and social media comments
- Focusing on narrow market channels

Exercise 1: Tools to Boost the Catalyzing Mindset

1. Keep a focus on customers, whether the "customer" is a member, patient, student, interest group, colleague or taxpayer. Customers require careful monitoring and support. Retaining customers requires meeting newequirements and providing strong customer service. To keep customers a central focal point:

- Share positive feedback from customers
- Recognize those who deliver outstanding customer service
- Post customer data (market share, new customers, sales volume, response times etc.)
- Conduct and publish quarterly reviews of market trends
- Review and analyze customer concerns, return rates and order patterns
- Offer first hand customer experiences to non-customer facing personnel

2. Stimulate customer-centric thinking by asking:

- What delights our customers?
- What complaints or concerns have surfaced?
- What is the competition doing or planning?
- What bottlenecks or practices slow our service?
- What causes returns, dissatisfaction or warranty work?
- Who has provided service above and beyond the call of duty?
- What can boost customer retention?
- Are our pricing and policies appropriate?
- What new market segments can we pursue?
- What will enhance our brand and goodwill?
- What will improve cross-functional customer awareness and service?
- Are we as responsive as we should be?
- Do we have the information systems we need?

©2017. Enterprise Management Ltd. All Rights Reserved.

Exercise 2: Catalyzing Mindset Steps

Review the following steps to guide your analysis of the following provided situation.

Step One: Analyze internal variables impacting customer acquisition, service, and customer retention:

- Product or service quality
- Robust inventory levels, shipping speed, and reliability
- Pricing and quantity discount pricing
- Service/support levels including response times and customer satisfaction
- Design and packaging
- Level of flexibility and ability to customize
- Marketing plan and advertising placement
- Supply chain efficiencies and quality
- Internal customer service training
- Customer relationship management system
- Customer communication plan
- Policies and standards
    - How is customer service currently being monitored and measured?
    - Are measures balanced between qualitative and quantitative factors?
    - Are measures balanced between short- and long-term indicators?
    - Are the rewards for outstanding customer service meaningful and motivating?
    - Are individuals who indirectly support customers recognized in addition to individuals who have direct customer contact?
    - Are there organizational barriers hampering customer service?
    - Is our warranty better than the competition?

Step Two: Collect information on potential external issues:

- Customer information
    - New customer requirements or issues; new organizational strategy
    - New decision makers or buyers
    - Hard data insights
        - Questionnaires, customer surveys
        - Focus groups, user conferences, meetings
        - Mystery shoppers
        - Digital information (Annual Report, News releases)
        - Review contract length and scope
- Competitive pressures
    - New pricing
    - New product launches
    - Technological advances
    - New practices (bundles of services, inventory practices, incentives)
    - New entrants
    - Potential substitutions
- Demographic shifts
- Brand and goodwill
- Regulatory and tax policy changes impact customers

Step Three: Analyze Gaps and Opportunities

- Identify the critical internal and/or external issues
- Appoint a task force, team or person to explore ways to close any gaps or resolve issues with a clear charter for their authority level, resources, expectations and time line.

Step Four: Evaluate and Implement

- Evaluate alternatives for cost, impact, timeliness and sustainability.
- Develop an implementation plan
- Prepare a presentation for authorization
- Prepare internal and/or external communication plan

Putting the Steps to Work: Analyze the Following Situation

Analyze the following situation, using the steps above, and determine two key actions you will take to collect additional data or actions you would proposed to improve sales.

Two of the organization's top customers have reduced the size of their orders over the last nine months. The impact has reduced your manufacturing firm's market share and you ability to meet sales goals. You also note increases in warranty work, sales force turnover, e-commerce activity, pricing pressures and new global competition.

_____

_____

_____

_____

_____

Exercise 3: Applying the Catalyzing Mindset to Your Enterprise

1. Identify a current customer that you want to obtain, retain or expand the relationship.

    ▸ What services are currently offered?

    _____
    _____

    ▸ What will earn new business?

    _____
    _____

    ▸ What costs and benefits are expected? Are they being fully delivered?

    _____
    _____

    ▸ What new challenges or opportunities are they facing?

    _____
    _____

2. Evaluate the current relationship.

    ▸ How long has the relationship existed? What level of customization is needed? Has the customer's strategy or scope changed? Are there key personnel changes in either organization?

    _____
    _____
    _____
    _____

- How is customer service currently being measured? Do the metrics include quality, returns, timeliness, service, and responsiveness? What additional factors should be monitored?

  _____
  _____
  _____
  _____

- What feedback have you received? What information do you need? What have you learned from focus groups, interviews, surveys, response cards, special events, advisory boards, user meetings, customer panels, Internet bulletin boards, or pilots?

  _____
  _____
  _____
  _____

- When was the last personal visit or call? Is it time to reconnect? Who should reach out to them?

  _____
  _____
  _____
  _____

3. Identify strategies to win new customers or strengthen an existing relationship:
   - Product/service customization or branding
   - Integrated customer service
   - Pricing and discounts
   - Just-in-time delivery
   - Integrated customer service

- Pricing and discounts
- Promotional opportunities
- Marketing support
- Greater automation
- Technical support
- Data sharing
- Communication strategy
- Mobile access
- Training customer's employees
- Retention budget
- Interact on social media
- Frequent buyer program
- Host or co-host an event
- Alignment based on values
- On-site personnel
- Dedicate point of contact
- Commission structure

Evaluate options aboce and select three or four for further analysis. Criteria should include: cost, time for impact, required manpower, sustainability, risks including impact on other customers, training requirements, expected return and any legal issues.

_____

_____

_____

_____

4. Prepare at least two targeted strategies for implementation including budget, personnel, benefits, time frame and goals/measures of success.

_____

_____

Exercise 4: Influencing a Catalyzing Mindset

What would you do to influence thinking in this situation?

Senior management is convinced that reduced sales are due to a service complaints and shipment issues. They recognize that service complaints are five times more likely result in customer loss than pricing or quality concerns. However, you believe that greater attention must be paid to research and development to offer new state-of-the-art products. You have asked for a R&D budget increase since new technology is showing great promise. However, senior management wants all available resources dedicated to customer acquisition and retention.

1. Circle the three phrases below that are most likely to be influentce senior management's Catalyzing Mindset:

    Market share, infrastructure, systems, state-of-the-art, accountabilities, efficiency, standards, risk reduction, innovation, brand, tradition, teamwork, competencies, alliances, best practices, collaboration, revolutionary, customer service

2. Write an opening statement that will capture management's attention and support based on their current Catalyzing Mindset Priority.

    _____

    _____

    _____

    _____

    _____

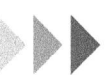 ## Deploying the Developing Mindset

The Developing Mindset focuses on establishing: the right balance between control and autonomy, setting polices to guide performance and implementing systems to achieve goals. Tailoring infrastructure, accountabilities and policies is an on-going task as technology, competitive forces and workforce expectations change. In fact, the search for the perfect structure might appear to be "accordion management" where the organization shifts between centralization and decentralization. Organization design requires: careful attention to job descriptions, reward systems, performance standards, compensation practices, cross-functional integration, staffing levels, facility planning, geographic reach, budget allocations, workforce planning, reporting systems, and goal alignment.

Organizational structures of today demand too much from a few, and not much at all from everyone else.
—GARY HAMEL

The neglected leadership role is the designer of the ship.
—PETER SENGE

Reflection

▸ What conditions stimulate your Developing Mindset?
_____
_____

▸ What can you do to stimulate the Developing Mindset in others?
_____
_____

The Developing Mindset can be encouraged by:
▸ Testing the effectiveness of operating systems and policies
▸ Examining internal collaboration
▸ Pushing decision making to the lowest appropriate level
▸ Aligning efforts through an integrated communication plan
▸ Reviewing resource allocation (staff, facilities, and budget)
▸ Updating promotion policies and career ladders
▸ Re-assessing pay policies
▸ Applying technology to speed information exchange

- Validating the effectiveness of the current organization structure
- Confirming reward policy effectiveness and use
- Establishing cross-functional task forces and networks
- Updating job descriptions, duties, and accountabilities
- Ensuring effective goal monitoring and measurement
- Increasing governance transparency
- Anticipating growth (staff, facilities, systems, capital expenses)

It is also wise to address any potential barriers to the Developing Mindset by avoiding:
- Concentrating on short-term issues
- Rewarding crisis management without addressing underlying cause
- Constantly restructuring systems and reporting relationships
- Assuming that "everyone knows what to do"
- Assigning work consistently to the "high performing units" to avoid weaker units
- Ignoring infrastructure gaps and silos
- Ignoring the need for risk analysis or customization
- Failing to update benchmarks, job descriptions, systems, and policies

Exercise 1: Tools to Boost the Developing Mindset

1. Manage expectations based on the level of expertise and the type of situation. When variables are known, a greater degree of authority is expected and reporting is less frequent and might even wait until after action has been completed. Less freedom or authority to act is appropriate when facing precedent setting, ambiguous, high risk, or high profile decisions. In these instances, review or consultation is required before action is taken.

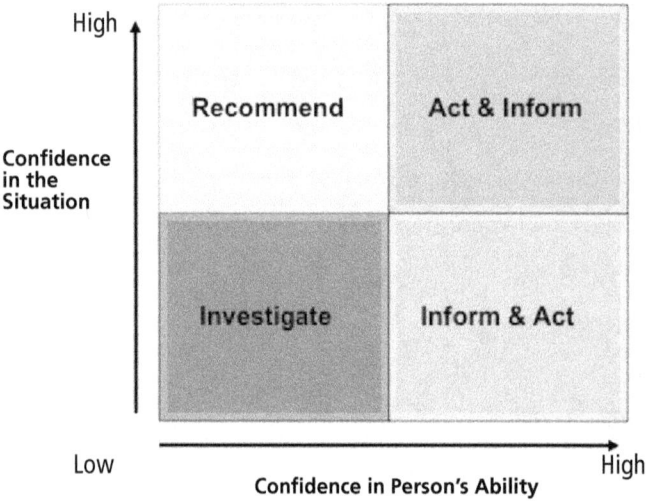

2. Ensure that operational metrics are comprehensive and appropriate. Consider the following factors:
   - Are qualitative and quantitative data included?
   - Are final metrics and interim, or in process metrics, being monitored?
   - Do the metrics cover all six Situational Mindsets?
   - Do the metrics cover all the areas that are subject to your control?
   - Are the metrics timely and useful?
   - Are metrics shared at all relevant levels?
   - What metrics can be added to ensure goals are balanced and achieved?

3. Check your personal time management.
- Record how you want to allocate your time as a percentage. Consider planning, managing, working on personal assignments, attending meetings, expanding your network, personal learning, coaching/mentoring, strategic thinking and other desired activities.
- For one week, assess how you spend your time by recording your daily activities in 15- or 30-minute intervals.
- Identify the variance between expectations and actual use.
- Identify your options using the following considerations; include others that are relevant to your situation/goals.
  - How much of your time is spent checking performance instead of providing performance standards/criteria and specifying reporting requirements?
  - How much of your time is spent resolving individual problems instead of tackling and removing organizational performance barriers?
  - How much of your time is spent handling conflict instead of developing the skills of others through coaching, sharing best practices, training, and managing knowledge?

Exercise 2: Developing Mindset Steps

Step One: Evaluate the current structure using the following factors in addition to those currently in use:

- Are goals clear and realistic?
- Does the staffing level enable timely communication, learning, and performance?
- Is there a line of sight or control over accountabilities?
- Is the unit effectively connected within the organization?
- Has an appropriate level of autonomy been delegated?
- Does the workforce have the requisite resources to meet its goals?
- Are skills, reports, and knowledge being continually updated?
- Do policies and systems support alignment?
- Does the group regularly reflect and learn from experience?
- Are teams truly interdependent or is every group called a team?
- Are organizational audits or reviews conducted at regular intervals to assess effectiveness, measure risk and communicate best practices?
- Is short- and long-term planning effective?
- Additional factors

_____

_____

Step Two: While there may be a tendency to ascribe poor performance to morale, consider organizational factors first. They are more likely to be the cause. Evaluate the following:

- Structure and clear goals
- Staffing or resource constraints
- Confused expectations or goals
- Sub-optimization or identification of unit goals at the expense of organizational goals
- Contradictory policies
- Insufficient pay or reward practices
- Cross-functional problems or weak collaboration
- Inadequate communication or system support
- Unrealistic or imbalanced work load
- Poor implementation planning
- Lack of access to decision makers or experts
- Inadequate training or knowledge
- Insufficient orientation and on-boarding of new employees
- Additional factors

_____

_____

Step Three: Identify actions you would recommend? What would you tackle first?

_____

_____

_____

_____

Step Four: What can be done to avoid similar occurrences in the future? What preventive measures, early-warning signals, changes in systems or practices, new policies and accountabilities could avert future problems?

_____

_____

_____

_____

Putting the Steps to Work: Analyze the Following Situation

Your organization seeks to improve on-time shipment to customers. A solution is needed for the short- and long-term. Sales have grown rapidly after positive press coverage. It has meant that new staff, facilities and equipment are needed. Initially, overtime was increased to meet an increased production schedule. However, last quarter there was a 1% decrease in productivity. Shipping schedules are slipping and customers are complaining. The VP of Sales is pointing a finger at Operations, while the VP of Operations is complaining that many of the new orders require customization and the sales force is promising unrealistic delivery schedules. The VP of Operations offered to provide partial shipments until new machinery is installed and new staff is fully trained. The VP of Sales has rejected the idea fearing it will result in lost sales and upset the sales force. Sales ommission payments would be delayed with partial shipments. Currently, commission checks are only paid after the order has been paid in full. Both VPs are requesting additional staff and budgets.

What three actions would you recommend? What would you do first?

_____

_____

_____

_____

_____

_____

Exercise 3: Applying the Developing Mindset to Your Team

Teamwork pays significant dividends. However, teams require structure, clear expectations and support. Use the following checklist to determine whether your team charter is completely effective. Consider the following factors and determine whether the factor is fully met (F), partially met (P), requires attention (RA) or not applicable (NA). Finally, identify what steps you might take to improve your team's effectiveness.

Step One: Mission and Goals

___ Are goals and mission clear and actively supported?

___ Are expected outcomes clearly established and understood?

___ Are measures of success and performance standards defined?

___ Do the measures cover quality, quantity, collaboration, suggestions, and timeliness?

Step Two: Context or Background

___ Are the business challenges and context discussed?

___ Are team resources, team sponsor, work systems, and goals known?

___ Is cross-functional collaboration specified and measured?

___ Are reporting relationships clear?

___ Are internal and external resources appropriate?

Step Three: Team Membership

___ What criteria drives team member selection?

___ Is the team size appropriate for the task?

___ Do team members understand why they were selected and how much time they are expected to devote to the team?

___ How are new members integrated?

Step Four: Authority

___ Is the team's level of authority clear and appropriate for the task?

___ Will authority or delegation levels change over time?

___ In what instances should the team seek guidance and from whom?

___ Is organizational support available to the team?

Step Five: Operations

___ Are team responsibilities appointed and updated?

___ What new roles or accountabilities will be needed?

___ How effective are team meetings? Are they held at appropriate times?

___ Has a quorum for a meeting been established?

___ How are suggestions evaluated?

___ How is quality assured?

___ What reports are expected and in what format?

___ What is the process for adding, ending, or changing assignments?

___ How is performance monitored and managed?

Step Six: Performance or measurement

___ What are the standards of performance?

___ Who reviews performance?

___ What are the measures of success?

___ How are data collected? From whom?

___ How are internal team operations evaluated and improved?

___ Is individual, team, and unit performance measured and rewarded?

___ Is feedback effective and two-way?

Step Seven: What steps can you take to improve your team's effectiveness?

_____

_____

_____

_____

_____

_____

Exercise 4: Influencing the Developing Mindset

What would you do to influence thinking in this situation?

Your mature West Coast organization just acquired a small East Coast start-up firm, which has an amazing entrepreneurial culture and exciting new products. Executives have been concentrating on merging systems, combining policies and practices, examining staffing levels and ensuring efficiencies. So far their decisions rely on established West Coast systems and policies. As the VP of Human Talent, you are concerned that the sought after entrepreneurial culture will be diluted by imposing West Coast practices. You believe that parts of the East Coast culture should be transplanted to the West Coast, since it is likely to position the organization for the future, retain top talent, and update competencies. Unfortunately, executives are focusing only on finishing the merger as quickly as possible using a Developing Mindset. and overlooking a Protecting Mindset.

1. Circle the three phrases below that are most likely to be influential:

   Market share, infrastructure, systems, state-of-the-art, accountabilities, efficiency, trends, risk reduction, innovation, brand, tradition, competencies, alliances, best practices, revolutionary, customer service

2. Write an opening statement that will capture management's attention and support based on their current Developing Mindset Priority.

   _____

   _____

   _____

   _____

   _____

   _____

©2017. Enterprise Management Ltd. All Rights Reserved.

Understanding the Performing Mindset

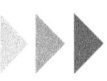

The Performing Mindset seeks to leverage performance data to improve worklfow, operating procedures, and boost financial return. This Mindset analyzes accepted approaches in an effort to improve quality, increase efficiencies, reduce performance variance, improve productivity and maximize resource use.

The Performing Mindset would not jump to conclusions. When asked the question: How long was the Hundred Years War? This Mindset would have looked up the data rather than rely on the duration stated in the name. The war actually lasted 116 years.

"One homerun is much better than two doubles."
—STEVE JOBS

"What gets measured, gets done."
—ANONYMOUS

Reflection

▸ What conditions stimulate your Performing Mindset?

_____

_____

▸ What can you do to stimulate the Performing Mindset thinking in others?

_____

_____

The Performing Mindset can be encouraged in teams and groups by:
- Collecting information on best practices
- Identifying gaps or barriers to streamline processes
- Conducting lessons learned reviews to leverage experience
- Reviewing performance standards and processes
- Posting and tracking team performance data
- Encouraging ideas to improve work flow or procedures
- Verifying effective safety practices
- Examining ways to improve profitability and profit margins

- Monitoring and improving resource utilization
- Allocating and adjusting resources to meet key needs and opportunities (budget, staff, equipment)
- Identifying the effectiveness, balance and relevance of current metrics
- Stressing the importance of, timely data in decision making

It is also wise to remove potential barriers to employing the Performing Mindset by:
- Ensuring that timely information is available and timely
- Addressing concerns that process improvement could reduce job security
- Requiring a high level of internal collaboration and lateral communications
- Clarifying output expectations
- Avoiding reliance on habit, past practice, or extreme "analysis paralysis"
- Reviewing documentation, training, and job aids to ensure that they are up-to-date
- Prohibiting sole focus on constraints (time, staff, budget, review cycle, workload)

Exercise 1: Tools to Boost the Performing Mindset

- Root Cause Analysis: Improvements result from addressing an underlying cause, rather than obvious symptoms.
  - Ask WHY five times before you jump into problem solving. It is likely that early analysis focuses on symptoms, not the root cause. While symptoms are noticed by their impact on costs, only by dealing with the basic problem, rather than symptoms, can the issue be permanently resolved. After each WHY question is answered, ask WHY again. Repeat the question to dig deeply for the root cause.
  - Root causes are rarely simple and frequently involve multiple factors. Check the following variables to fully detect the root cause:
    - Methods or standard operating procedures
    - Material or suppliers
    - Money
    - Systems
    - Equipment
    - Facilities
    - Human resources/staffing/skills

- Individual performance problems should proceed from those issues that are easy to fix and them move to those that require greater time and effort. This analysis should start immediately when a

  problem surfaces. The following sequence enables you to address the easier to solve issues before confronting the more challenging problems:
  - Is the person physically able to perform the job?
  - Does the person have the necessary equipment/tools, information, and space to meet expectations?
  - Is there a problem with materials or supplies?
  - Is there confusion over expectations, standards, or schedule?
  - Does the person understand the process and have the necessary training to do the job?
  - Are there organizational barriers, constraints, or gaps that affect performance?
  - Is there a lack of essential willingness/motivation to do the job?

- Proactively address potential risks and ramifications to prevent derailment. Consider the following factors:
  - Have we adequately addressed standards, monitoring process, metrics, and support level that will enable early detection of deviations?
  - What will improve our systems, practices robustness, and resilience?
  - How realistic are our schedule sand resource levels?
  - What will avert future problems?
  - What new skills, job aids, or training is needed?

Exercise 2: Performing Mindset Steps

Step One: Examine areas for improved workflow, productivity, quality, procedures, efficiency, and safety. ITechnology, knowledge, materials, and specification changes should be analyzed..

Use the list below to prioritize areas for analysis. Identify each area as potentially High, Medium or Low using the letters H, M, and L.

___ Staffing levels and work schedules

___ Training/competency mastery

___ Recruitment, orientation, and training

___ Resource allocation

___ Machinery/equipment

___ Layout/space/facilities

___ Supply chain and reliable vendors

___ Shipping
___ Reporting process
___ Material/input
___ Methodology/procedures/workflow
___ Maintenance schedule and effectiveness
___ Performance standards
___ Cross-functional collaboration
___ Management and cooperation
___ Information exchanges
___ Documentation/record keeping

Step Two: Collect data on high priority areas identified above. Consult with others, while maintaining an open mind. Probe for information and solicit suggestions for improvement.

Step Three: Establish a process for evaluating data, identifying alternatives and assessing feasible solutions. Allocate time to check for potential ramifications and risks of proposed solutions.

Step Four: Select the most promising alternatives and develop an implementation plan. Prepare a proposal for authorization.

Step Five: Implement the plan with balanced metrics to ensure success and prevent surprises. Confirm that the following areas are appropriately addressed:

- Innovation measurements: Innovation such as the number of suggestions offered, percentage of output from a new process/product, or the number of new synergies.
- Customer or client measurements: Examples are the level of customer satisfaction, the retention rate, or willingness to provide references, testimonials, or support.
- Systems measures: Collaboration such as the ability to work with other units, the number of lateral networks, effective decision delegation, or the willingness to share best practices.
- Process measures: Quality or financial measures such as the return on assets, the number of defects, the amount of waste, or output per hour.
- People measures: People satisfaction and growth such as the level of cross training, increased skill levels, staff retention rates, or internal promotion rate.
- Strategic measures: Evidence of strategic thinking including the ability to identify strategic opportunities and threats, use of problem avoidance and prevention, attention to defining "what business we are in," and the ability to integrate technology.

Step Six: Monitor and measure improvements to ensure that the expected gains have been achieved as expected.

Putting the Steps to Work: Analyze the Following Situation

A six-year old health care supplier has grown dramatically through aggressive pricing as well as meeting quality standards. Two years ago they expanded by building three new facilities near their major customers, obtaining new vendors, and hiring local staff. While in the past the firm primarily relied on promotion from within, recently MBA graduates have been hired. Recently, operating costs have escalated and given the already low profit margins, this trend must be reversed. The largest problem is at the newer facilities. You recently finished your MBA and is seen as an "independent. thinker." Therefore, you have been asked to analyze current operations and identify ways to bring costs under control.

What three areas would you plan to investigate? Where would you start?

_____

_____

_____

_____

_____

Exercise 3: Applying the Performing Mindset to Your Enterprise

1. Identify an opportunity to improve existing practices, work flow or performance standards. If an opportunity does not immediately surface, consider the following:

    ▸ Do organizational interrelationships effectively support productivity?

    _____

    _____

    ▸ Are the formal and informal systems aligned to ensure high levels of performance?

    _____

    _____

    ▸ Are goals and expectations realistic, specific, challenging, measurable, and time bound?

    _____

    _____

    ▸ Does documentation and reporting meet current needs?

    _____

    _____

    ▸ Are lessons learned from past projects identified and best practices implemented?

    _____

    _____

    ▸ Are benchmarks used effectively?

    _____

    _____

2. Consult with others to confirm your analysis.

3. Collect internal and external data. Research relevant benchmarks and best practices.

   _____
   _____
   _____

4. Ask yourself and others:

   ▸ What should we start doing?

   _____
   _____

   ▸ What should we stop doing?

   _____
   _____

   ▸ What should we do more often?

   _____
   _____

   ▸ What should we do less often?

   _____
   _____

   ▸ What would make us truly outstanding?

   _____
   _____

5. Evaluate the alternatives and select the most promising for implementation.

   _____
   _____
   _____

6. Prepare a proposal for implementation outlining the issue, the solution, the benefits, the risks and the costs.

_____
_____
_____
_____
_____
_____
_____

Exercise 4: Influencing a Performing Mindset

What would you do to influence thinking in this situation?

Your VP has started setting plans and goals for the new fiscal year. Your department wants to capture new Millennial customers. Recent trends indicate that this would be a smart move to position the firm for the future. It would require an investment in new mobile technology. However, you know that the VP is focusing on improving ROI by reducing costs and improving productivity. A new mobile initiative might be seen as too expensive and risky given the firm's cost pressures. Yet, it would also grow the customer base. On the other hand, overhead costs for mobile technology are projected to be far cheaper than existing processes.

1. Circle the three phrases below that would mostly like gain the VP's attention and support:

    Position for the future, customer service, profit margins, accountability, economies of scale, standards, competitive edge, innovation, tradition, teamwork, competencies, quick return, boost the brand

2. Write a persuasive opening statement targeting the Performing Mindset to introduce the idea of expanding your market niche to include Millennials.

_____
_____
_____
_____
_____
_____

Deploying the Protecting Mindset

The Protecting Mindset concentrates on workforce culture, talent, and retention. A skilled and committed workforce is essential to an organization's success. This Mindset focuses on developing competencies, supporting teamwork, and building an adaptable culture to meet changing requirements. Much like a magnetized iron bar that lifts twelve times its weight; people who are committed, respected and dedicated deliver significantly greater results. To magnetize people, the Protecting Mindset delivers coaching, a sense of accomplishment, teamwork, pride, respect, information, trust, and support. It also ensures continued succeess through succession planning, new competency development, and engagement.

"Culture eats strategy for breakfast."
—PETER DRUCKER

Reflection

- What conditions stimulate your Protecting Mindset?

  _____
  _____

- What can you do to stimulate the Protecting Mindset in others?

  _____
  _____

The Protecting Mindset can be encouraged by:
- Soliciting ideas from across a wide spectrum of viewpoints/perspectives
- Requiring collaboration, team work and information sharing
- Demonstrating trust
- Recognizing ideas, participation, and contributions
- Setting a standard of civility and respect
- Handling conflict constructively
- Setting outcome expectations
- Praising performance and initiative
- Offering relevant training, job aids and resources
- Requesting feedback
- Providing performance and career coaching

- Leveraging non-verbal cues
- Establishing a safe culture where assumptions, concerns, and interests can be discussed
- Summarizing agreements and action plans
- Hiring for cultural match as well as talent match
- Supporting organization values and mission
- Developing a change ready culture

It is also wise to remove any potential barriers to commitment and esprit d' corps such as:
- Withholding key information
- Ascribing blame for mistakes or derailments
- Practicing micro-management
- Displaying favoritism in assignments or promotions
- Permitting cliques to exist
- Encouraging competition among team members
- Ignoring poor performance, disrespect, or information hoarding
- Insisting that the leader must approve every decisions

Exercise 1: Tools to Boost the Protecting Mindset

1. Workforce Skill Management: Skills must keep pace with new challenges. A highly competent staff increases organizational flexibillity. Check the following areas for potential improvement:

- Are new skills, knowledge, or practices for the future being developed?
- Are relevant development opportunities available to all employees?
- Are training needs regularly assessed?
- Are training programs effectively targeted and is learning effectively transferred to the job?
- Are employees cross-trained for key positions?
- Is continuous learning supported?
- Do employees have and act on their development plan?
- Are developmental records kept up to date?
- Is continual learning a key criteria for promotion?
- Are managers held accountable for performance counseling and career coaching?
- Is there a workforce/succession plan for key positions?
- Are developmental assignments and activities used appropriately?
- Do employees know how to implement change?

© 2017. Enterprise Management Ltd. All Rights Reserved.

2. Developing a high performing culture: Assess the strength of your culture in terms of performance, teamwork, commitment, agility and preparedness for the future. How would you rate your culture on the following:

- Offering greater autonomy in making routine job-related decisions
- Providing challenging work
- Using creative ideas and suggestions
- Recognizing strong performance
- Providing appropriate job security
- Ensuring an effective work-life balance
- Enhancing collaboration and teaming
- Increasing knowledge and expertise
- Understanding and supporting career goals
- Providing appropriate job variety
- Developing critical thinking practices
- Offering feedback and guidance
- Eliminating internal competition
- Encouraging trust, respect, and inclusion
- Accessing support or help when needed
- Sharing internal and external information
- Developing change readiness
- Rewarding adaptability and resilience
- Listening to issues, concerns and suggestions
- Working closely with customers, clients, and subject matter experts

Exercise 2: Protecting Mindset Steps

Step One: When coaching, consider motivational drivers using McClelland's motivational framework. McClelland's three drivers are: performing challenging work (achievement motivation), belonging to a group or team (affiliation motivation), or having the power to influence action (power motivation). Motivational descriptions are:

- Achievement oriented people are motivated by challenging work and professional improvement. They seek assignments where they can strive for excellence. Their motto is "the best and nothing else."

- Affiliation motivated people value being team members pulling together for a common goal. Their motto is "united we stand, divided we fall."

- Power motivated people seek impact and action through persuasion, organizational insight, inspiration and goal setting. Their motto is "lead, follow or get out of the way."

Step Two: Prepare for the coaching session by identifying how to recognize high performance. Suggestions include:

- Achievement driven: assign interesting projects, provide opportunity to present work to others, recommend potential mentors, request expert opinions, and offer individual assignments.

- Affiliation driven: share information, offer feedback, solicit ideas, express gratitude, write complimentary notes, and celebrate team accomplishments

- Power driven: assign "acting" title when out of the office, provide opportunity to shadow key personnel, appoint to lead a task force, and provide visibility up the chain of command.

Step Three: Reflect on how you and the organization can contribute to the person's development.

Step Four: Write or practice your opening statement in front of a mirror and watch for non-verbal signals.

Step Five: Set up a meeting for the presentation. Be sure to clarify the purpose and ask the person to think about their strengths, interests, and suggestions.

Step Six: Ask the person for their assessment of their strengths and areas they would like to ehance or learn, since everyone can improve. Comment as appropriate. Discuss developmental ideas or actions.

Step Seven: Document a plan for the future. Establish milestones and metrics.

Putting the Steps to Work: Analyze the Following Situation

You have just been assigned a new unit to manage, which is in addition to your existing three units. The new unit's manager has recently retired and his replacement, Bob, has just been promoted. His promotion was from team member to team manager and it has been difficult. Bob has taken many management courses but is struggling with the challenge of transitioning from being a colleague on the team to a manager of the team. Team performance has slipped recently. Bob has always displayed commitment and a willingness to help others. He is a team players and a good listener. However, he may be letting weaker performance slip. You want to help him and the team be successful. You need to act quickly. A new strategic thrust will be announced shortly that will put the team under more presssure. And, it will require new competencies and practices.

- What motivation currently drives Bob?

  _____

  _____

- What support can you offer? What actions are needed?

  _____

  _____

- What would you say to start the session and ensure Bob does not become defensive?

  _____

  _____

- Identify three issues you would raise while also displaying confidence in his skills and abilities.

  _____

  _____

- What would you avoid doing or saying during your first meeting with Bob?

  _____

  _____

Exercise 3: Applying the Protecting Mindset

Reflect on your personal career goals. Recognize that career growth includes expanding abilities and responsibilities in a current position, making lateral moves, and upward advancement.

Step One: Identify areas for development by responding to the questions below:

- What new skills and/or experiences will be required in the future?
  _____
  _____

- What are your long-term interests and aspirations?
  _____
  _____

- What brings you the greatest satisfaction? What type of work environment do you prefer?
  _____
  _____

- How can you align more effectively with the organization's strategy?
  _____
  _____

Step Two: Analyze opportunities.

- Analyze promotional practices: Who has recently been promoted? Why were they promoted? Consider whether the promotion was: (1) vertical or lateral and (2) technical/specialization or general management focused.
  _____
  _____

- What skills or experiences do you need to develop in your current position or for your next step? Be sure to consider internal training, attendance at external events/university programs/conferences, temporary assignments, reading, self-study, job rotation, shadowing, mentoring, certifications/degrees and special assignments.
  _____
  _____

©2017. Enterprise Management Ltd. All Rights Reserved.

Step Three: Develop a six to twelve month career development plan.

- What two possible career moves match your interests and plans?
  _____
  _____

- What data or information do you need to confirm your plans?
  _____
  _____

- Do the potential position matchs your values and preferences? Will the work environment meet your needs?
  _____
  _____

- Does your plan align with organizational strategy and goals?
  _____
  _____

- Which potential position do you prefer and consider likely? _____
  _____
  _____

- What resources are available?
  _____
  _____

- Is the developmental plan realistic, time specific, and likely to garner support?
  _____
  _____

- Who could effectively serve as your mentor or coach?
  _____

▸ Who could fill your position upon your advancement? Finding your replacement is key to being able to leave your current position.

_____

_____

▸ Whose support is needed to implement your development plan?

_____

_____

Step Four: Discuss the plan with those whose support is critical to successful implementation:

1. Set an appointment for the meeting, identify the agenda as feedback on your career development plan, and specify that you are seeking feedback and suggestions. Identify and be ready to answer potential concerns or questions that might arise.

   _____

   _____

2. Prepare a written plan for discussion and prepare your opening statement.

   _____

   _____

3. Listen for suggestions and confirm next steps.

Exercise 4: Influencing the Protecting Mindset

What would you do to influence thinking in this situation?

A highly experienced operational team has focused on productivity for many years. They are proud of supporting the "brand" and have perfected their processes, quality, and standards. They know they contribute to the "bottom-line." Due to new competition and technology, the organization has decided to discontinue the team's product line. You must encourage Susan, the team's manager, to shift from a Performing Mindset to a Protecting MIndset to help the team prepare for this shift. You know that she is currently focus on hard data, productivity, and quality. However to adjust to the upcoming changes, she must accept a shift from achievement and outcome focus to buidling a team for future challenges. She needs to know that she is has to deliver different results.

1. Which three phrases below would you focus on in the conversation?

    Fast growth, new markets, job security, customer service, loyalty, state-of-the-art products, accountabilities, efficiency, standards, respect, risk reduction, innovation, collaboration, change readiness, profit, metrics

2. Draft the first two sentences that you will use to start a constructive conversation to gain her support for the upcoming changes and help her accept her new responsibilities.

    _____
    _____
    _____
    _____
    _____
    _____
    _____

# Deploying the Challenging Mindset

The Challenging Mindset targets sustainability, learning from experience, and seizing new opportunities. Existing operational assumptions are retested, since they can erode over time. New risks can develop undetected unless there is a regular environmental scan. Asking questions such as "What business are we in?" may appear to be rhetorical but, in reality, it is relevant in our fast-changing world. New niches can develop and customer preferences can change. Sustainable organizations must let go of established business models and comfortable routines to prepare for the future. The future is where we will all spend the rest of our lives.

"The dogmas of the quiet past are inadequate to the stormy present. The occasion is piled high with difficulty, and we must rise to the occasion. As our case is new, so we must think anew and act anew."
—ABRAHAM LINCOLN, Second State of the Union Address

"It is not the strongest of the species that survive, nor the most intelligent, but the one most responsive to change."
—CHARLES DARWIN

Reflection

▶ What conditions stimulate your Challenging Mindset?

_____

_____

▶ What can you do to stimulate the Challenging Mindset in others?

_____

_____

The Challenging Mindset can be encouraged through:

- Sharing information on industry trends
- Examining economic and product cycles
- Holding lessons learned exercises from recent projects
- Testing operating assumptions to ensure their current relevance
- Identifying and institutionalizing best practices
- Conducting a SWOT analysis
- Identifying the best case, worst case and likely case for new ventures
- Exploring new market niches

- Encouraging the use of "devil's advocate" to test for risk and consequences
- Using sub-groups to avoid "group think"
- Exploring potential new partnerships and alliances
- Using force field analysis to evaluate new initiatives

It is also wise to remove any potential barriers to employing the Challenging Mindset by:
- Providing time to analyze risks and opportunities
- Requiring your team to use the Mindset Checklist before jumping to a decision
- Insisting that three or more solutions or initiatives are identified for consideration
- Ensuring that out-of-the-box thinking is praised
- Revising your business model to meet new trends
- Exploring options for new potential alliances and partnerships
- Conductin after action reports or lesson learned exercises

Exercise 1: Tools to Boost the Challenging Mindset

1. Prepare for the future by developing a deep understanding of emerging opportunities. To capture trends, investigate the following to ensure a sustainable future.
   - Analyze data trends within your organization.
   - Examine trends in your industry, business or discipline as well as trends in government, society, workforce and technology.
   - Read material unrelated or parallel to your professional discipline, attend meetings/conferences, and discuss trends with knowledgeable experts as well as novices.
   - Examine business events in unrelated areas for potential impact. Most organizations find their new competitors are non-traditional ones.
   - Review future predictions for potential new strategic insights.
   - Collect information and suggestions from front-line employees

2. Encourage the use of the devil's advocate approach. Knowing the potential drawbacks and risks improves decision quality and prevents missteps.
   - Identify your intention to contribute to the decision making process by assuming a devil's advocate role.
   - Ask the group to consider ramifications, risks, and assumptions knowing that awareness can prevent problems or reduce their impact.
   - Probe for additional ideas, solutions, initiatives and partners.

Exercise 2: Challenging Mindset Steps

Force Field Analysis aids effective decision making, planning, and gaining authorization for change, since it looks at the case for and against an initiative.

Step One: Identify a change initiative or opportunity.

_____
_____
_____
_____

Step Two: Explore the internal and external drivers that support the initiative.

_____
_____
_____
_____

Step Three: What are the potential responses or sources of resistance? Consider past change initiatives to reveal potential areas of esistance that might appear immediately or over time.

_____
_____
_____
_____

Step Four: Identify additional driving factors that would increase support for this change initiative.

_____
_____
_____
_____

Step Five: Determine what will reduce or eliminate resisting forces. Note that addressing current resisting forces is frequently overlooked, even though it is one of the most effective ways to increase support and promote successful implementation.

_____

_____

_____

_____

Step Six: After reviewing the forces for change and the forces that will resist change., determine if, the change is appropriate at this time. Does this initiative require additional consideration, data collection or pilot testing before making a final decision?

_____

_____

_____

_____

Putting the Steps to Work: Analyze the Following Situation

Situation: A respected service provider has decided to re-organize changing from a functional organization (Operations, Sales, Finance and Accounting, Administration-facilities and HR, Legal, Marketing) to a customer focused matrix organization. The goal is to effectively utilize specialized expertise, increase customer focus and stir innovation. The organization has operated primarily in the Mid-West and wants to organically expand across the US. The workforce has extended tenure, a high level of autonomy, dual track career growth (managerial and specialized expert career options) and a new president with a strong sales background. The former president was from Operations. Since this will be a significant organizational and strategic change, a clear understanding of the pro's and con's is necessary. Use the steps above to conduct a Force Field Analysis to identify the driving and resisting forces.

Exercise 3: Applying the Challenging Mindset

Conduct a SWOT analysis to analyze internal strengths (S) and weaknesses (W) as well as external opportunities (O) and threats (T) in your organization/unit.

Step One: List your current internal strengths by reviewing the following questions:

- What are our primary assets?
- Do we have a strong and united organization/team?
- Are we operating effectively and without silos?
- What expertise or talents do we have?
- What produces high levels of performance?
- What best practices are being used?
- What do we do well?

_____

_____

Step Two: Examine the weaknesses or current limitations by probing:

- What must we improve?
- Are there resource constraints?
- What system limitations or barriers exist?
- Are we limited by our policies, practices, people, equipment, systems, or structure?
- Does low levels of autonomy, trust, or collaboration limit productivity?
- Do we have the facilities and locations we need?
- Do we have the talent and skills we need for the future?
- Do we learn from our experiences?
- What operating or business model changes are needed?

_____

_____

Step Three: Identify the external opportunities that are evident or emerging by asking:

- What economic, social, technological, or regulatory trends will sustain our success?
- What external factors present new opportunities?
- Where are beating our competition?
- Are we leveraging the newest or best technology?
- How can we serve our customers more effectively?

© 2017. Enterprise Management Ltd. All Rights Reserved.

- What new customers can we serve?
- What can build our brand or reputation with our customers and community?
- Are there "low hanging fruit" opportunities?

_____

_____

Step Four: Identify current and potential external threats by reviewing the following questions:
- What external obstacles or barriers confront us?
- What limits our success?
- What are others doing that we are not?
- What new threats are likely?
- What short- or long-term trends or risks might impact us?
- What might impact our brand or reputation?
- What assumptions may no longer be valid?

_____

_____

Step Five: Identify an initiative based on the SWOT analysis that will capitalize on internal strengths, mitigate weaknesses, capture external opportunities, and deflate threats.

_____

_____

_____

_____

Step Six: Share your SWOT analysis with others and ask for additional input and insights.

_____

_____

_____

_____

Exercise 4: Influencing the Challenging Mindset

What would you do to influence thinking in this situation?

You are the Operations Director in charge of a mature product line that produces 30% of the organization's revenue, despite having a low profit margin. Your organization's current large customers like to do business with you because you have an extensive product line and inventory. The new CEO is considering focusing on products with higher profit margins. He might decide to drop older products, including yours. You think this may significantly impact customer retention, reduce revenue, and impact morale. You want to influence the CEO's strategy. You recognize that the CEO is currently operating from a Challenging Mindset.

1. Circle three phrases that would help you gain his support for reconsidering the option.

    Sustainable future, job satisfaction, quality, accountabilities, efficiency, employee development, brand/reputation, risk reduction, collaboration, customer trends, infrastructure, business model, succession planning

2. Draft two sentences that you will use to open a conversation with the CEO.

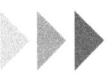# Working with Others: Influencing, Conflict Management, Teambuilding and Mindset Checklist

Influencing

Influencing does not require personal charisma or charm. And it is not a matter of formal power. Influence is the ability to see a goal and enlist the support of others by communicating how the desired action will be a win-win opportunity. Influence relies on understanding the customer, having strong connections or networks, identifying goals and benefits, and offering incentives, all of which can be developed and applied easily. The activities below will demystify the influencing process. It is not a matter of what you know or what is "logical" that is important. It is a choice you make. The bottom line is working with others to achieve mutually satisfying goals.

The ability to sway opinions and decisions without using force or coercion is important in gaining authorization for initiatives and/or support for implementation. By understanding another person's Situational Mindsets, you can present ideas that will gain support and develop a win-win solution.

Step One: Increase your ability to influence by reviewing your effectiveness in the following areas:

1. Credibility: Ask others if you have met their expectations or what you can do to meet their expectations. What can you do to increase your effectiveness? How can you improve the perception of your commitment to follow through on agreed actions?

   _____
   _____

2. Competence: Identify what skills, experience, and knowledge would increase your ability to influence others.

   _____
   _____

3. Flexibility: Adaptability comes from a broad information base and situational awareneess. What can you do to increase your access to information? What questions can you ask to determine the appropriate level of flexibility? How well do you communicate the need for situational agility?

   _____
   _____

4. Mindset Alignment: How can you improve your ability to idenitify current Mindsets? How comfortable are you in starting conversations using multiple Mindsets?

_____
_____

5. Connections: Who would you like to have in your network? What do you do to maintain your network? Who could you mentor? Who could become your mentor?

_____
_____

6. Common Goals: How can you communicate your goals to others to gain their support? Do you listen and understand the goals presented by others? Can you identify the areas are negotiable and those that are non-negotiable? How well can you identify or create mutually satisfying goals?

_____
_____

7. Active Support: What level of support is needed? Whose support is critical? What concerns or issues might limit commitment? What issues need to be addressed? What modifications can increase active support? What signals separate compliance from true commitment and engagement?

_____
_____

8. Communication Effectiveness: Is communication flowing downward, laterally and upward? Is it timely and accurate? Are multiple communication modes being employed? Is there a communication plan? What in the following list will improve communication?

    ▸ Gaining attention/interest by discussing the case for change
    ▸ Soliciting input, suggestions and ideas early in the decision making process
    ▸ Listening to positions, concerns, and reactions with an open mind
    ▸ Communicating benefits from each Mindset's point of view
    ▸ Clarifying next steps and expectations and ensuring that they are fully understood and accepted
    ▸ Communicating progress and achievements regularly
    ▸ Praising progress to maintain momentum
    ▸ Celebating success and recognizing contributions

© 2017. Enterprise Management Ltd. All Rights Reserved.

Step Two: Designing an Influential Communication Plan

1. Identify a person whose authorization or support would help you achieve your goals. What do you want from that person?

   _____
   _____

2. What is your goal or objective?

   _____
   _____

3. What are the benefits of your proposal?

   _____
   _____

4. What are the other person's goals?

   _____
   _____

5. What are the outcomes the other party seeks?

   _____
   _____

6. After gathering information, what is that person's probable Mindset? Is your assessment confirmed by referring to the Mindset Predictor from page 4.

   _____
   _____

7. What can you do to satisfy the other person's Mindsets or desired outcomes?

   _____
   _____

8. Review the Mindset goals, approaches and limitations from your Leadership Spectrum Report. You may choose to use the following outline.

    Compatible Goal: What is a win-win goal?
    _____
    _____

    Mutual Focus: What shared interests should be emphasized?
    _____
    _____

    Common Approach: How should the discussion be opened?
    _____
    _____

    Aligned Expectations: What outcomes are reasonable, given the other person's Mindset?
    _____
    _____

9. What is the optimum setting and timing?
    _____
    _____

10. What are realistic next steps?
    _____
    _____

© 2017. Enterprise Management Ltd. All Rights Reserved.

Managing Conflict

Conflict can be constructive as well as destructive. Productive conflict frequently reveals new ideas, draws attention to emerging risks, and ensures that all points of view are aligned. However, it can also negatively impact performance and harm personal relationships. Dysfunctional conflict frequently consumes 20 percent of a manager's time. Effectively handling unproductive conflict reduces distractions and encourages collaboration.

Conflicts start with objective differences over actions someone has taken or the goals they are pursuing. These disagreemenet can be addressed objectively. When they become tense, disagreements turn into conflict and become subjective as it shifts away from actions and goals. Unproductive conflict centers on personality, rather than goals or decisions. When conflict jumps to stereotypes or attributions, such as the other person has an agenda, it is difficult to defuse or resolve. The earlier unproductive pesonality based conflict is addressed the less damage will be done.

Objective Disgareement Management

Step One: Explore the facts driving each point of view.
- Collect factual data using open-ended question
- Summarize hard data and facts
- Separate subjective conclusions or untested assumptions from factual information

_____

_____

_____

Step Two: Summarize the facts and explore proposed solutions.
- Discuss new information
- Identify negotiable and any non-negotiable aspects
- Explore potential resolutions or solutions
- Identify at least three solutions for discussion and evaluation

_____

_____

Step Three: Consider each alternative solution:
- What are the desired goals or outcomes?
- What is the expected impact?
- What resistance might surface?
- How does the proposal fit into the larger picture/context?
- What are the trade-offs, ramifications, and risks?
- What is the best solution at this time?
- What level of support will it garner?
- Is the support level sufficient for implementation?
- Who needs to authorize?
- What resources are required and available?

Step Four: Develop an Implementation Plan
- What are the mutual goals?
- What are the measures of success?
- Who will lead? Whose support is essential?
- What is the timeline?
- What are the key milestones and performance expectations?
- What resources will be allocated?
- What support will be given?
- Who will monitor?
- What must be avoided?
- What is the communication plan?

Subjective Conflict Management

When disagreements on actions and goals are not managed, personal conflict and emotions develop. To manage these situations it is important to remain calm, manage stress levels, listen carefully and observe non-verbal clues. If emotions are high, meet with the parties individually before holding a joint conversation.

Some tips for handling these situations include:
- Be respectful to all points of view
- Focus on the present since you cannot change the past
- Deal with one issue at a time
- Concentrate on specifics and avoid generalizations

- Maintain an open mind
- Avoid labels, accusations, stereotypes or blame

To handle subjective conflict consider the following steps:

Step One: Start with a full understanding of the situation from the point of view of the person who brings the issue to you.

- What would he/she like to start doing as a result of the situation?
- What would he/she like to do more frequently?
- What would he/she like to stop doing?
- What would he/she like to change about the level or type of system support?
- What resolution is desired?

Step Two: Develop a plan:

- What facts are accepted by all parties?
- What goals are shared?
- What areas are open for discussion or exploration?
- What creative alternatives or synergies are possible?
- What is the cost of no resolution?
- What information should be share with both parties before a joint meeting?

Step Three: Jointly explore alternatives solutions and the related costs and benefits. Listen to new ideas. Select a fair resolution that can be sustained in the short- and long-term.

Step Four: Mutually agree to a plan of action and document it for mutual review.

Step Five: Confirm the understanding, agree to milestones, and establish check points. Agree to an implementation process.

Step Six: Communicate to relevant parties for agreement, authorization, or implementation.

Step Seven: Follow up on the agreement and make necessary modifications.

Building Team Effectiveness

1. Share the six Situational Mindsets with your team and discuss how each contributes to smarter choices. Be sure to discuss how each adds value and ensure that all are used for complex or difficult decisions. Discuss how the Mindset Checklist can be used to support critical thinking.
2. Ask the team to focus on one situation and identify the factors that currently drive their thinking. Connect the criteria to a Mindset and ask if there are any Mindsets that are being overlooked.
3. Discuss the value of having different Mindsets as well as common Mindset on the team Different Mindsets slow decision making and may lead to tension, while aligned Mindsets may lead to group think and blind spots.
4. Explore the general strengths and potential limitations of a team having common Mindsets using the informaiton below.

Team Mindsets common patterns reflect potential team strengths and potential liabilities as the team faces complex, challenging, or precedent setting issues. The four predominate patterns are described below:

When the Mindset Priorities concentrates in Developing and Performing Mindsets, it indicates likely:

Strengths

- Strong achievement orientation
- Understands structure and systems
- Monitors and measures progress

Potential Limitations

- Narrow measures of success
- Internal focus
- Reliance on tested ideas and incremental change

When there is alignment around the Inventing and Challenging Mindsets patterns might be:

Strengths

- New ideas or initiatives
- Supports rapid change
- Collaboration and frank exchanges

Potential Limitations

- Ignoring systems or system constraints
- Overlooking details amid enthusiasm
- Unrealistically optimistic

When Inventing and Catalyzing Mindsets dominate thinking, the potential impact is:

Strengths

- Achieving new successes
- Getting things right
- Exploring options

Potential Limitations

- Weak follow-through
- Poorly analyzed details
- Failure to meet deadlines

A Protecting and Performing Mindset pattern reveals likely:

Strengths

- Getting things done
- Understanding procedures, systems, and culture
- Sustaining work flow and success

Potential Limitations

- Rely on established policies
- Resist "unnecessary" change
- Underestimate external factors

Situational Mindset Checklist

Situations that are complex, ambiguous, or ground breaking require careful consideration. The *Situational* Mindset Checklist lists key questions that must be explored to ensure that all aspects are fully understood and leveraged for effective analysis and smart analysis. Teams can tailor this list for their specific situation, client base, industry, goals, and responsibilities.

Inventing

1. How can we encourage "out of the box" thinking?
2. What alternatives are there?
3. What can be synthesized across functions, disciplines, product lines, or service offerings?
4. Do we identify multiple options before we settle into analyzing and evaluating them?
5. If there were no constraints, what could we do?
6. What is the ideal product or service?
7. How can we take our existing procedures/methods to a new level?
8. What technologies can we leverage more fully?
9. What insights might surface if we sought the opposite results?
10. What has never been tried before?
11. What have we given up on in the past that might be viable now?

Catalyzing

1. Are we meeting our goals?
2. What new customer niche can we serve?
3. What are customers saying about us?
4. Who is the competition?
5. How can we increase our commitment to our customers?
6. What retains our customer base?
7. Who can is the best person to handle a customer issue?
8. Who has produced results?
9. What will increase our responsiveness?
10. What will give us a competitive edge?
11. How can we improve our response time?

Developing

1. What is expected of us? What is the plan?
2. How should we organize?

© 2017. Enterprise Management Ltd. All Rights Reserved.

3. How do we balance centralization and decentralization?
4. How do we balance autonomy and control?
5. How should information flow?
6. What policy or systems are necessary to achieve our goals?
7. How will accountabilities be delegated?
8. What new systems are necessary? What systems need to be re-evaluated?
9. How can we consistently deliver excellent results?
10. How can we avoid confusion?
11. How should resources be allocated?

Performing

1. What will it cost?
2. Is it practical?
3. Do we have the resources?
4. What are the deadlines?
5. Are our processes effective?
6. How can we improve our processes?
7. How can we reduce costs?
8. What are the best measures?
9. What data are missing?
10. How can we improve results? What analysis is needed? (re-work, errors, cycle time, resource usage)
11. Where can we leverage our resources more effectively?

Protecting

1. What are the risks and ramifications?
2. What are the benefits?
3. What is fair?
4. Who needs to know or approve?
5. Have we heard from everyone?
6. How can we reward performance?
7. How can we develop people?
8. What planning can be done for succession?
9. Is this consistent with our culture, traditions, or values?

10. Who can help develop talent?
11. How has this been handled in the past? Is this part of our culture?
12. What develops our core competencies?

Challenging

1. What assumptions may no longer be valid? Are we resting on our reputation?
2. What non-traditional threats could arise?
3. How can we more effectively balance short- and long-term goals?
4. How can we achieve broader goals?
5. What opportunities are there?
6. How can we address our weaknesses?
7. What would we do if we were to start all over again?
8. How can we increase our flexibility?
9. How can technology help us?
10. What are the emerging customer expectations and trends?
11. Are there symptoms of "group think?"
12. Are we effectively using the lessons we have learned?

Mindset Predictor responses from page 5:
1. Inv, 2. Pro, 3. Dev, 4. Per, 5. Chal, 6. Per, 7. Inv, 8. Pro, 9. Chal, 10. Cat, 11. Dev, 12. Chal, 13. Inv, 14. Per, 15. Inv

© 2017. Enterprise Management Ltd. All Rights Reserved.

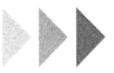

Additional Resources

Enterprise Management Limited offers two training programs to apply the *Situational* Mindsets to promote brilliant analysis and achievements. *Situational* Mindsets: Delivering Brilliant Results targets individuals, while the Risk and Opportunity Practicum targets teams. Please contact us at info@entereprisemgt.com for further information.

The *Situational* Mindsets program prepares leaders for today's rapidly changing customer, marketplace, workforce, and technology by developing mental agility, critical thinking and wise decision-making. This program presents the Situational Mindset model for making the right call at the right time to deliver the right results. Getting it right from the start saves time, resources and goodwill. Leveraging current circumstances, avoiding pitfalls and seizing opportunities requires more than being in the right place at the right time. It requires analysis using the *Situational* Mindset Checklist, wisdom to implement change and active support.

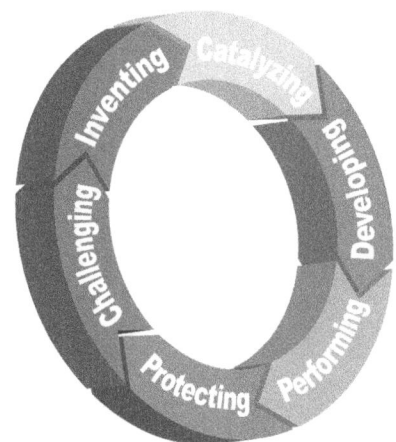

The Risk and Opportunity Practicum enables a team of four to five unit members to analyze and improve outcomes. Each team will collect data and analyze current performance. Based on their analysis, the team will then identify opportunities for improvement and present their proposed recommendations to management. Since the team developed the initiative based on unit data, initiative implementation proceeds smoothly.

This program is a "practicum" because it is hands on. Half of the session focuses on learning and analyzing and the other half is devoted to guiding each team to design an improvement initiative for their unit.

For futther information, please contact Enterprise Management Limited by email at info@enterprisemgt.com or visit the website at www.enterprisemgt.com.

www.ingramcontent.com/pod-product-compliance
Lightning Source LLC
Chambersburg PA
CBHW080520300426
44112CB00018B/2808